THE WILL TO FAIL

Kevin L. Michel

FROM KEVIN L. MICHEL

Steam Over Cold Steel

Acta Non Verba: Deeds, not words

The Will to Become

The Four Upgrades: Reprogram Your Mind, Mood, Memory, and Meaning

The Council of Gods

Shadow-Dialogues at the Edge of Reason

Refractions of the Real: A Manual for Self-Directed Beings

A Book for the Fragmented Who Seek to Become Whole

The Little Green Book of Guaranteed Success

Moving Through Parallel Worlds To Achieve Your Dreams: The Epic Guide To Unlimited Power

CONTENTS

PROLOGUE

Y ou are holding a confession wrapped in a dare. Everything you are about to read will strip away the excuses you have polished through the years, those polite stories that let you sleep after sabotaging your own chances. This book was forged to bully your comforts, to drag your quiet betrayals into open daylight and watch them smolder. You will not enjoy every paragraph, yet you will feel a pulse of recognition in each one, the throb that signals a buried truth striking bone.

Look around your life, the cluttered ambitions, the half-finished plans, the relationships bruised by needless conflict. These are not accidents. They are deliberate monuments to a hidden loyalty you pledged long ago, the loyalty to keep yourself small because small feels safe. You misnamed that loyalty

as fate, circumstance, personality. It is none of those. It is a decision, signed in secrecy, renewed every time you hesitate, scroll, binge, ghost, or lash out.

This book calls that decision what it is: **the will to fail**. Nietzsche saw it when he warned that a warlike spirit, starved of worthy battles, will turn its weapons inward. Freud saw it in the death drive, the compulsion to crash against the same wall until the impact feels like home. Modern neuroscience traces it in the dopamine spikes that reward your impulsive escapes and leave your long-term goals starving. You will see it too, once the pages ahead pry your eyes open.

Do not look for gentle affirmations here. Affirmations coddle, they cushion, they lull you back to sleep. You need the opposite. You need a verbal alarm that rattles the windows, forcing you upright at three in the morning when complacency usually tucks you in. This prologue is that alarm. It rings to announce: the door to your prison cell is already open, your ankle chains are unlocked, yet you stand motionless, hugging the rusted bars because their chill is familiar.

You will walk out of that cell only when the disgust of staying outweighs the fear of leaving. This book was designed to load that disgust with voltage. Each chapter will confront one more payoff you secretly harvest from failure: the false comfort, the ready sympathy, the tidy identity of the perennial underdog. You will see how those payoffs bleed you dry. Then you will learn the opposite habit set, the rituals that keep craftsmen, athletes, and trailblazers charging forward while the rest of the world watches from the bleachers.

You have been warned. Turning the next page is an act of treason against your old loyalties. It will cost you the privilege of complaint, the camaraderie of shared mediocrity, the opioid calm of low expectations. What you will gain is unfiltered authority over yourself. Authority hurts at first. It places every outcome, good or bad, squarely on your shoulders. Yet authority is the only soil in which greatness ever grows.

If you accept the terms, read on. Lock eyes with your own reflection in these sentences and refuse to look away until the shame turns into resolve. The forge is hot, the hammer is raised. Step forward. Offer the raw iron of your life. The blows will come either way. Better they come with purpose.

The choice is yours, and it begins now.

PART I – SLAPPING THE MYTH AWAKE

CHAPTER 1:
FAILURE IS A
DECISION

Y ou stand in the wreckage of yet another failure and wonder, "How did this happen *to* me?" The harsh truth is it didn't just *happen* – you *chose* it. Every time you've fallen short, some part of you was a willing accomplice. Failure is not mere bad luck or lack of ability; failure is a decision. It's a decision you made in the shadows of your mind, perhaps without conscious intent, but a decision nonetheless. This may be a slap in the face, but it's time to slap the myth awake: the myth that you are an innocent bystander in your own downfall. You are not. You are the author of your failures, writing them into existence one self-sabotaging choice at a time.

Think back to the critical moments you've bungled – the exam you blew because you "accidentally" procrastinated all night, the job opportunity you lost because you mysteriously got sick on the interview day, the relationship you torpedoed because you picked a pointless fight. Are these just unfortunate coincidences? Or were they decisions, made by a part of you that wanted out, wanted an excuse, wanted to fail? Be brutally honest: you decided to fail, and then you executed that decision with precision. You stayed out partying before the big exam. You "forgot" to set your alarm for the interview. You pushed your partner's buttons knowing it would explode the peace. These were not mistakes; they were choices. Your choices.

You might be recoiling right now, thinking No, I truly wanted to succeed! On the surface, yes – your conscious mind yearns for success. But underneath, in the murky depths of your psyche, there lurks another agenda. Psychologists have long noted this split: one part of you drives toward the goal, while another sneaky part applies the brakes and swerves off the road. That second part is your inner saboteur, and it quietly says, "No, succeeding is a terrible idea." It then stealthily orchestrates a failure, leaving you kicking yourself later, wondering what went wrong. The cruel joke is that it was your own mind that wrecked you – your own decision to mess up, even if it was a subconscious decision.

It's hard to accept that you have been complicit in your defeats. Society tells us to soothe our egos: "Don't be too hard on yourself. You did your best. Circumstances were against you." But let's be blunt – often that's a lie. You weren't against the ropes; you were against yourself. You made the decision to retreat, to underperform, to fail – because on some level, failing felt safer or easier than winning. This isn't about blame for blame's sake; it's about ownership. If you don't own your failures, you can't own your successes either. As long as you believe the myth that failure just happens to you, you'll remain its victim. The first step out of this trap is to face the mirror and say: I chose to fail. Not to beat yourself up, but to reclaim your power. Because if your choices got you here, then your choices can get you out.

Throughout history, sharp observers of human behavior have noticed this self-destructive streak. Friedrich Nietzsche noted that, "Under conditions of peace the warlike man attacks himself.". Think about that. When life served you peace or the potential for real progress, did you grow uneasy and pick a fight with yourself? When things were going well, did you suddenly do something stupid to ruin it? That is exactly what Nietzsche meant. Deprived of external battles, you created an internal one. You manufactured a crisis or a failure because some part of you only feels alive in struggle. So if no enemy is at the gates, you become your own enemy.

Sound familiar? It should. When you had a stretch of calm or success, didn't you find a way to mess it up? A flourishing romance that you sabotaged with baseless jealousy, a steady job you sabotaged by slacking off or stirring drama, a healthy streak you broke with a binge – these are your internal warlike instincts turning on yourself in the absence of external threats. It was a decision, however hidden, to attack your own well-being.

Let's drop any remaining illusions. You are not cursed by fate, nor simply sabotaged by others – you have been choosing failure. You decided to stay in your comfort zone when growth beckoned, you decided to take the shortcut knowing it would dead-end, you decided to indulge in the habits that eat you alive. Each decision was a tiny vote for failure. And all those votes accumulated into the life you have now.

This realization is not meant to make you feel worthless – it's meant to make you feel powerful. Why? Because if your life is the product of your decisions, then a better life is the product of better decisions. You had the power to choose defeat; which means you also have the power to choose victory. But to wield that power, you must first acknowledge it. No more shrugging and saying "I don't know why

I keep failing." You do know. You fail because you decided to. Own that fully.

Now, you might ask: Why on earth would I ever decide to fail? I want to be happy, successful, respected! On a rational level, yes, of course. But humans aren't purely rational beings. We're driven by hidden currents – fears, desires, instincts – that can directly oppose our conscious goals. To truly wake up and change, you need to understand those hidden currents. You need to know why your brain, your very own brain, would betray you and crave ruin over triumph. This is where we dive deeper – into the psychology, the neurology, the deep recesses of the mind. Brace yourself for Part I, Chapter 2, where we'll expose why some brains (including yours) actually crave failure. Only by dragging these tendencies into the light can you begin to fight back.

You made the decision to fail. Now, let's find out why you did – and how to stop making that damning choice ever again.

CHAPTER 2: WHY SOME BRAINS CRAVE RUIN

It sounds perverse, doesn't it? The idea that your brain might *want* to fail. After all, on the surface you seek success and happiness. But as we've established, beneath the surface lurks another agenda. Why would any brain crave ruin, chaos, or pain? To answer this, we must confront some uncomfortable truths about human psychology – truths identified by great thinkers like Freud and Nietzsche, and supported by modern neuroscience. Prepare to meet the darker drives inside you, laid bare.

Over a century ago, Sigmund Freud proposed a chilling concept: an inborn "death instinct" –

Thanatos – an unconscious drive toward destruction, self-sabotage, and ruin. In Freud's view, all living beings carry this lurking impulse to return to an inorganic state, to essentially annihilate the self. It stands in opposition to *Eros*, the life instinct that drives us toward survival, creativity, and connection. This isn't just academic psycho-babble; you can observe it in your own life. Think of those inexplicable urges to wreck something going well, or the strange comfort you sometimes find in negative emotions. Freud would say that's Thanatos whispering in your ear, nudging you toward self-destruction.

Freud noticed that people often repeat painful or destructive behaviors with almost compulsive consistency – what he called the repetition compulsion. Trauma survivors, for example, might reenact their trauma in various ways; those who have been hurt seek situations to be hurt again, as if drawn by a magnet of pain. Sound familiar? Perhaps you always date the same toxic type of partner, or you always sabotage a job just when you're up for promotion – different scenarios, same self-defeating script. Freud's theory was that an unconscious force – a death drive – is behind this, making you seek the familiar pain over the unfamiliar peace.

Modern psychology echoes these observations. The term "repetition compulsion" is used to describe how people *keep* engaging in behaviors or relationships that replicate old hurts, even though it causes them suffering. It's as if the mind is caught in a loop, chasing the ghosts of the past. Why? Perhaps in hopes of a different outcome, or simply because the brain finds comfort in the known, even if the known is misery. If you grew up in chaos or abuse, calm stability as an adult might actually feel *wrong*, and so you (without even realizing it) stir up the chaos again – because *normality* feels abnormal to you.

Think of your brain as having a thermostat for chaos and pain – this is your comfort zone, twisted as that sounds. If your baseline expectation is that life is full of struggle and disappointment, then when things get *too good* or *too calm*, your inner thermostat says "This isn't right" and kicks on the AC of self-sabotage to bring you back down to the familiar cold. Psychologists have noted how people will sabotage their own success due to a "fear of success," which is really a fear of change and of leaving one's comfort zone. The truth behind a lot of self-sabotage is that you're afraid of what success will do to your comfortable, predictable life – so you avoid the new, unsettling situation that big success would bring.

Nietzsche's insight intersects here: "Under conditions of peace, the warlike man attacks himself." When your external world has no conflict, your internal world manufactures it. Some part of your brain *craves* the battle. That warlike spirit needs an enemy, and if none is handy, it will turn you against you. Have you noticed that when life is going smoothly, you start to feel uneasy, even *bored*? Maybe you start overthinking trivial problems or inventing issues out of thin air. That's the warlike brain seeking its fix of struggle. Peace feels foreign, even intolerable, so the mind says, "Time to stir up trouble!" And down you go, attacking yourself to satisfy an inner craving for conflict or drama.

Many people who've lived through chaos actually find peace *unsettling*. One survivor of a chaotic upbringing confessed, "When chaos really is all you know...stability is actually unsettling." She described unconsciously sabotaging stability in her life because calm felt wrong – if everything was going well, she would *create* a problem just to restore the chaos she was used to. She admitted, *"My mind is an expert at creating problems that really aren't there."* Does that strike a chord with you? Have you not done the same – created issues where none existed, simply because a part of you felt more comfortable in conflict?

There is a twisted *comfort* in ruin for some brains. Imagine a prisoner who has been locked up for so long that freedom scares him. He might commit a new crime just to go back to the familiarity of jail. In psychology, this is known as being "institutionalized." Well, you can become institutionalized in *failure*. Your brain, having become used to disappointment and chaos, actually starts to prefer it. It's what you know. It's your prison cell, but at least you recognize every wall. Success, on the other hand, is unknown territory – new expectations, potential embarrassment, the fear of falling from a higher height. So your brain says, "Let's stick to what we're good at: failing."

Hard to believe? Consider this: Comfort in chaos is a real addiction. Therapists have noted "chaos addiction" in which people *find comfort and familiarity in disorderly or chaotic situations*. Peace strikes them as strange; they feel uneasy when things are calm. To mask inner pain or simply out of habit, they *seek out* instability and drama. They'll pick a fight, sabotage a project, or chase some dangerous thrill just to create the turbulence that feels like home. And afterward, they often face the very failures (broken relationships, lost jobs, personal wreckage) that on some level they were aiming for all along. It's chaos for the sake of chaos, ruin for the sake of familiarity.

Let's dig even deeper into the brain's wiring. Neurologically, a big piece of this puzzle is dopamine – the neurotransmitter of desire, motivation, and reward. Modern neuroscience, has shown how dopamine drives our behaviors. We often think dopamine equals *pleasure*, but more accurately it equals *wanting*. It's the itch that demands scratching. It peaks when we anticipate a reward or experience novelty. Now consider: chaos, conflict, or the dramatic downfall *is* a kind of perverse reward for a craving brain. It's intense, it's stimulating, it's *something happening*. Your conscious mind hates the failure, but some unconscious part of you is like an addict getting its fix of intensity. That surge of adrenaline and emotion when you gamble your success and lose – there was a twisted dopamine rush in the build-up. Some brains prefer that spike of *Oh crap, here we go again* over the steady hum of stable progress.

In fact, giving in to self-sabotaging behavior often

provides immediate relief or gratification, even as it ensures long-term failure. Procrastinate on an important task – what happens in the moment? You feel relief: *Ah, I don't have to stress about it now.* That's a quick dopamine hit for avoiding pain. Skip your workout and binge TV instead – immediate comfort (dopamine rewards you for energy conservation and entertainment). Blow up at someone instead of calmly resolving an issue – immediate emotional release (ah, the catharsis of drama). The *long-term* consequence of all these is negative, but your brain's reward circuits aren't concerned with long-term; they crave the *now*. So your primitive brain can literally *want* these self-defeating choices because they satisfy something right now: comfort, release, stimulation. In doing so, it inadvertently pushes you toward failure. As neuroscientists have pointed out, stacking quick dopamine hits through such behaviors inevitably leads to a crash – a state of diminished motivation and poor performance. In other words, chasing short-term fixes makes you underperform in the long run. Your brain's short-sighted cravings set you up to fail.

Let's also talk about fear – fear of success, fear of happiness, fear of the unknown. These fears often masquerade as self-sabotage. Perhaps deep down you believe you don't deserve success or happiness (maybe instilled by childhood experiences or trauma), so when you get close to it, you'll do something to ruin it, aligning reality with your internal self-image of unworthiness. Psychologists note that self-sabotage is frequently a protective mechanism, rooted in fear and self-doubt. Your psyche thinks it's protecting you – from the vulnerability of hope, from potential disappointment, from leaving people behind, from having to live up to more. So it trips you before you run too far. It's twisted logic: *"Better to crash the plane myself than risk an unpredictable accident later."* This is how your brain rationalizes ruin.

Summing it up: your brain craves ruin because on some primitive, misguided level, ruin *feels right*. It feels safe, familiar, or rewarding to the deeper layers of your psyche. The death drive drags you toward self-destruction. The repetition compulsion makes you reenact old failures. The warlike instinct seeks battle and finds it in self-battle when life is peaceful. Habitual chaos comforts you while calm makes you uneasy. Quick dopamine hits lure you into choices that undermine you later. Fear of the unknown keeps you clinging to the devil you know.

This is a grim inventory of human tendencies, but we are dragging them into the light for a reason: so you can finally see your enemy. When you understand *why* you've been choosing failure, you can begin to outmaneuver these internal forces. Knowledge is power – now you know that your brain's craving for ruin is not a moral failing, but a perversion of natural drives. That means it's something you can work with and change. There is an opposite set of drives – call it the life instinct, the creative urge, the will to forge (as we'll later name it) – that you can strengthen to overcome the will to fail.

Before we get there, though, we must confront something else: the insidious *benefits* you've been getting from your failures. Yes, benefits. As sick as it sounds, your self-sabotage has been feeding you psychological payoffs that kept you hooked. We need to expose those payoffs and rip them from your hands. Only a fool gives up an addiction without understanding what they're getting out of it. So in *Part II: The Hidden Payoffs*, we will examine how failure has been comforting you, shaping your identity, and otherwise rewarding you – and why you must reject those false rewards. Ready to dig even deeper? Let's go.

PART II – THE HIDDEN PAYOFFS

CHAPTER 3: COMFORT OF THE CELL

Picture a prisoner who has spent decades locked up. Finally, he's up for parole – freedom is at hand. But instead of rejoicing, he's terrified. Outside those prison walls lies the unknown: new responsibilities, no structure, possible failure at life out there. In here, in the cell, it may be miserable, but it's *predictable*. It's *safe* in its own twisted way. So he does something unbelievable: he commits a small violent act just to ruin his parole chances. He chooses to stay caged, because the cage is comfortable compared to the anxiety of freedom.

Now realize: *you have been that prisoner.* Your cage is your pattern of failures, your comfort zone of underachievement and self-sabotage. It may be painful, but it's *predictable pain*. And predictability breeds comfort. This is the comfort of the cell – the hidden payoff of failure that keeps you coming back for more.

Every time you fail, you retreat to a familiar place: the bottom. Sure, it's not where you outwardly want to be, but there's a perverse relief in being there. When you're at the bottom, there are no expectations to fulfill, no further to fall. You can say, "Oh well, this is just how I am. Nothing more to lose." There's a lullaby of comfort in that state. You wrap yourself in the cozy blanket of self-pity and *no one can hurt you further* because you've beaten them to it. You've preemptively put yourself in the cell so the world can't throw you in. Safe, in a backward way.

Let's break down the elements of this comfort:

Firstly, failure removes pressure. Success is pressure – it raises the bar, invites attention, sets expectations for next time. But if you consistently fail or stay mediocre, the pressure's off. No one's expecting great things from you (they might feel sorry for you instead, which sadly can feel easier to handle than high expectations). You avoid the weight of responsibility that comes with success. There's comfort in that lightness. It's the "nothing to lose" mentality. As twisted as it is, part of you finds it relaxing that people just shrug at your endeavors. If you announce you're going to run a marathon or start a business, *then* people will watch and maybe expect results. Scary, right? If you never try or you publicly quit, people leave you alone. That's comfortable.

Secondly, failure can be used as an *excuse* to avoid even scarier possibilities. If you fail on your own terms, you never have to face the question of whether you *truly* measure up. A classic example is the student who parties the night before an exam and fails. On the surface, a failure – but he can console himself, "I failed because I didn't try hard. If I *had* tried, maybe I'd have nailed it. My potential is still intact." This is textbook self-handicapping: you deliberately sabotage your performance so that your ego stays safe – any failure can be blamed on the circumstances you created, not your inherent ability. It's strangely comforting to fail with an excuse, rather than risk trying your best and discovering that your best wasn't good enough. By not giving full effort, you protect the illusion, the comforting belief that *you could have succeeded if you really tried.* Thus, the cell of failure shields you from the harsher possibility of personal limitation. Researchers note that self-handicapping is a strategy we use to "avoid taking responsibility for our failures" by hurting our chances on purpose. We think it protects our self-esteem. It does, in the short run – but at the cost of growth and true achievement.

Think of how many times you've done this. Didn't study enough, didn't practice enough, procrastinated, showed up late – little sabotage moves that ensured you wouldn't succeed brilliantly, thereby giving you an out: *"Well, I failed, but it's only because I kind of slacked off... if I'd put in full effort, I'd have done great."* This false comfort has kept you returning to that behavior, because it's *easy* on the ego in the moment. But long-term it cements a self-image of incompetence.

Thirdly, failure often brings external comfort in the form of sympathy and help from others. When you screw up or fall apart, others may rush to console you, assist you, or at least they lower their expectations of you. You might not consciously *seek* pity, but there's a subtle payoff: being the underdog or the victim can feel validating in its own way. People tell you, "It's okay, it was a tough break, you did your best." You get emotional support, leniency, maybe even materially someone bails you out. If part of you craves care or fears standing on your own feet, failure can be a twisted method to get nurturance. It's like subconsciously saying, "If I fall, someone will catch me and give me attention." So you orchestrate a fall.

Be brutally honest: Have you ever leaned into a failure or a weakness because of the attention or compassion it brought? It's nothing to be proud of, but it's human. Perhaps you noticed that when you were struggling, friends gathered, but when you were doing well, they were distant or even envious. So you stay in struggle to maintain connections. Or your family only unites around crises – so you (unconsciously) contribute a crisis. These are hidden payoffs: failure as social glue or a call for love. Comforting, in a dysfunctional way.

Fourth, failing lets you stay in familiar territory, avoiding the fear of the unknown. Success is uncharted water. If you've always been in poverty, finally making money is scary – you don't know how to handle taxes, investments, new social status. If you've always been overweight and self-conscious, actually getting fit and attracting attention is terrifying – who *are* you if not "the fat funny one"? Better to stay in the known pain than venture into unknown pleasure. The devil you know is better than the devil you don't, as the saying goes. Well, some of us believe the heaven we don't know might hide a devil, so we stick with hell just to be safe. This mentality keeps you in your cell with the door wide open – free to leave, but unwilling to step out.

All these factors form a padded lining on your prison cell. They make the hard walls of failure feel softer, comfortable. But make no mistake, a comfortable prison is still a prison. The "comfort of the cell" is perhaps the most insidious reason you haven't broken out. Who wants to leave coziness for hardship? This is why you must reframe your perspective: that comfort is a poison. It is false comfort, like a drug that soothes you even as it kills you. It's the warmth that will lull you into never changing while your life passes by. You have to come to see the cell as *truly* uncomfortable – as stifling, as suffocating – even if you've decorated it with excuses and lowered expectations.

Start by examining the stories you tell yourself for comfort. "It's not my fault." "I'm unlucky." "I'm just not cut out for that kind of success." "At least I'm not as bad as so-and-so." "Someday, when I really try, I'll show them." These are your lullabies in the cell. They make you feel okay about not pushing harder today. They need to be stripped away. You need stark silence in that cell to finally realize *I don't want to live here anymore.* No more coddling your failure with nice narratives. Call it what it is: you settled for less because it was easier.

Consider also how you manage anxiety or fear. Everyone feels fear when stepping out of their comfort zone – the successful and the unsuccessful alike. The difference is what you do with it. If you keep choosing failure, chances are you have zero tolerance for the anxiety of change. At the first twinge of uncertainty, you retreat to safety (the cell). You must learn to tolerate that discomfort of growth, to see it as a positive sign. We will get to techniques for that in Part IV. But right now, just recognize the pattern: every time you avoided doing something that could improve your life because it made you anxious, you were seeking the comfort of the familiar failure instead. You basically said, "I prefer the certainty of being unhappy to the risk of being uncomfortable on the way to happiness." Let that sink in. It's pathetic, isn't it? And yet, so very human.

Here's a crucial realization: The comfort of failure is temporary, but the costs are permanent. Yes, you feel relief in the moment when you avoid the challenge, blame the excuse, or fall back into familiar misery. But the long-term weight on your heart – the knowledge that you're not living up to your potential, that gnawing regret – that is profoundly uncomfortable. It's the deep suffering you trade for shallow comfort. Over time, the cell gets colder, darker. What was once "not so bad" becomes a personal hell of stagnation. The sympathy from others fades as they tire of your self-pity. The excuses wear thin even to your own ears. Eventually, what was comfortable becomes intolerable. Don't wait for that eventuality. Break out now.

Before we move on, remember this: comfort is the enemy of growth. Those who achieve, who overcome, who self-actualize – they make a habit of doing what is uncomfortable. They willingly leave the cozy cell and wander in the open, where anything might happen. They trade false safety for true liberty. You must do the same if you want to escape the will to fail.

In the next chapter, we'll tackle another hidden payoff of failure that's closely tied to comfort: the way failure becomes entangled with your very identity. If comfort is the soft bed in your cell, identity is the chains that keep you tied to the bed. It's time to break those too.

CHAPTER 4: IDENTITY AS ANCHOR

W ho are you, really? It's a question we all grapple with, and many of us quietly settle on an identity that, while limiting, feels secure. Perhaps you've labeled yourself *the underachiever, the screw-up, the one who never catches a break.* It might not be flattering, but it's *yours.* It's consistent. And consistency in identity feels like an anchor in the chaotic seas of life. So what happens if life tries to pull you out of that identity? Often, you unconsciously sabotage the change to snap back to who you believe you are. Identity is one of the strongest anchors holding you in the sea of failure.

Humans will go to great lengths to behave in ways that confirm their identity and beliefs about themselves. If you deep-down believe you're not meant for success, you will find ways to ensure failure so that reality matches belief. It's uncomfortable to have a self-image (say, "I'm a failure") that doesn't align with external reality (say, you start succeeding wildly). Cognitive dissonance kicks in – that psychological discomfort when our self-concept and experience mismatch. To resolve it, either we change our self-concept (hard!), or we change our experience to align with our self-concept (often through sabotage). Most people choose the latter without realizing it.

Consider someone who has long identified as a victim of circumstance. It becomes a core part of their narrative: "Bad things just happen to me, I have the worst luck." Now imagine they suddenly get a great opportunity, things are going well – if they succeed, that narrative crumbles. So, what do they do? They might unconsciously ruin the opportunity, maintaining their identity as the perennial victim. Now they can comfortably say, "See? Told you. I just can't win. It's who I am." The failure, painful as it is, *reaffirms* their identity, which perversely gives them psychological comfort. They know who they are again.

Or think of someone who prides themselves on being humble, maybe to a fault. They fear that success would make them arrogant or that people would see them as egotistical. So to stay aligned with "I'm a humble underdog," they never let themselves win big. It's a hidden benefit: they get to keep saying, "Aw shucks, little old me, I'm nothing special," and feel modest and virtuous. But the cost is they hold themselves back from excellence.

Identity forms early and from many sources: your family, your culture, your past experiences. Perhaps your family drilled into you that "people like us never get ahead" or "money corrupts you" or "don't outshine your siblings." Such messages can root deep, making you *guilt-ridden* at the thought of surpassing those around you. Success then feels like a betrayal. Many people self-sabotage because of a misplaced sense of loyalty or fear of abandonment: *If I rise, will my friends/family still accept me?* If you grew up around failure or mediocrity, succeeding can mean leaving your tribe's comfort zone, and that triggers primal fear. So your identity as a member of that group holds you back – an anchor dragging on any upward momentum.

There's a known hidden barrier to success called the *disloyalty-abandonment belief:* the fear that achieving success will make you disloyal to your roots or cause you to be abandoned by those you love. For example, someone from a working-class background might sabotage their climb up the socioeconomic ladder because unconsciously they feel they'd be betraying their upbringing or making others look bad. They might fear that friends will envy or reject them. So, they stay "one of the guys/girls" – they stay the same. It feels safer, loyal, familiar. Their identity as that kid from the block remains intact, but at the cost of their dreams.

Your identity can also anchor you through *labels* you've embraced: "I have anxiety," "I'm ADHD," "I'm an introvert," "I'm a procrastinator," "I'm the black sheep," etc. While these labels can help you understand yourself, they can also become excuses. They become *what you are*, rather than *what you can overcome*. If you see these traits as immutable identity, you won't challenge them. You'll say, "Well, I procrastinate because I'm a procrastinator – it's just my nature." And thus, you give yourself a lifelong pass to continue the behavior. The label anchors you to the habit. Part of you might even take pride in the label, wearing it like armor: "This is just me, accept it." That pride makes it even harder to shed the behavior, because now your *ego* is tied up in it.

Even negative identities can provide a strange sense of pride or uniqueness. Being "the tragic, misunderstood genius who never got his break" or "the martyr who always sacrifices and suffers" can be alluring to the ego. It's like you're the star of your own drama. If you give up that identity, who are you? Just another normal person? The ego balks: *No, I am special in my suffering.* So you continue to unconsciously orchestrate scenarios that fit that special-suffering identity. You might reject practical help or solutions, because subconsciously you fear losing that narrative that sets you apart. It's an anchor chained straight to your pride.

Let's not forget the role of *group identities* as well. If you're part of a community or friend circle where everyone bonds over shared struggles (for instance, a group of friends that all hate their jobs and commiserate daily), success for you threatens group cohesion. If you suddenly love your career or start a thriving business, what happens to the gripe sessions? You might be excluded or you won't relate anymore. So to avoid rocking the boat, you unconsciously stay stuck. Your identity as a member of that complaining circle holds you at their level.

We also have identities around our capabilities: "I'm not a math person," "I'm creatively inept," "I'm terrible at relationships." These become self-fulfilling prophecies. Identify as "not a math person" and you'll avoid learning math or sabotage efforts – after all, it's not *you*. Identify as "terrible at relationships" and you'll behave in ways that ensure your relationships fail, because anything else doesn't jibe with who you *think* you are. The hidden payoff here is the comfort of consistency. You get to be right about yourself. Humans love being proven right, even if it's about negative things. It's weird but true. You'd rather be right that you're a failure than risk being wrong and facing an identity crisis.

So how do we break this anchor? First, by recognizing that *identity is a story* – and stories can be rewritten. You are not a static character doomed to replay the same role forever. You can choose a new role. In fact, you can choose to *not* tie your worth to any rigid identity at all. Identities should be tools, not prisons. For example, instead of "I'm a failure," reframe to "I have failed in the past, but that's not who I must remain. I can be someone who learns and grows." Instead of "I'm the one who never fit in," tell yourself "I am a work in progress and I will find where I belong as a healthier person."

Be warned: when you try to change, your old identity will fight back viciously. It will feel like an identity *crisis*, and indeed it is – the old self is fighting for its life. You might experience a void, a lost feeling: if I'm not that struggling person, who am I? That void is scary, but it's also potential – an empty field where you can build a new you. Don't rush to fill it with the same old junk out of fear. Stand in that discomfort. Realize that you are the forge, not the cast metal. You can melt down those old self-definitions and shape new ones.

It's okay – even necessary – to outgrow people and roles that keep you in failure. It might mean some relationships change or end. It might mean facing disapproval from those who preferred you "small." But consider: the ones truly in your corner will celebrate your positive changes (even if it takes them time to adjust), and the rest? They were chains, not friends. Would you really chain yourself forever just to please others? Don't answer with your habit; answer with your ideal self.

One more hidden payoff of identity-as-anchor: It gives a sense of *certainty*. Humans fear uncertainty. Knowing "I am a failure" is oddly certain – you know what you are, you know your lane. But life's one true constant is change and uncertainty. Embracing a better path means embracing the unknown. Your identity anchor resists that strongly. But remember, a ship anchored in harbor never discovers new lands. You have to pull up the anchor of who-you-used-to-be and let yourself voyage. Will there be storms? Sure. But stagnating in harbor (stuck in an old identity) guarantees you'll never grow.

To cast off this anchor, actively craft a new narrative about yourself that aligns with where you want to go, not where you were. For instance, start saying "I'm someone who is learning to succeed," "I'm becoming disciplined and focused," "I deserve good things as long as I work for them," "I can handle being happy and I won't abandon my true friends, nor will they abandon me for improving." These might feel false at first – that's natural because they conflict with your ingrained belief. But through repetition and *action* to back them up, they'll become true. You'll build evidence for the new identity.

Keep in mind: identity isn't just thought, it's action. Every time you take a new action (however small) that the old you wouldn't take, you chip away at the old identity and reinforce the new. For example, the "old you" would sleep in and skip the workout. The "new you" forces yourself up and exercises. That act, done consistently, sends a powerful message: I am now a person who prioritizes health and discipline. Over time, you truly become that person. The old identity loses its grip because your daily reality no longer validates it.

By shattering the hidden payoffs – the comfort and the identity – you remove two major incentives your subconscious had for keeping you stuck. You start to realize that *failing has no real payoff at all; it's a net loss.* What you thought were benefits were illusions. Comfort in stagnation turns into suffocation. Identity anchored in failure turns into shame. Good. Let it hurt. Let it outrage you. You should feel an inner rebellion now: "I don't want to be that person anymore. I refuse to stay comfortable in that filth. I refuse to cling to an identity that holds me down."

Hold onto that anger and determination. We will use it. In **Part III: How We Keep the Fire Lit**, we'll examine how you have been perpetuating the cycle of failure day-to-day – the tools of sabotage you employ and the social environment that reinforces your losing streak. It's time to snatch those tools out of your own hands and to break the unspoken agreements in your environment that love to keep you losing. Let's turn now to the nuts and bolts of self-sabotage and how to strip them down.

PART III – HOW WE KEEP THE FIRE LIT

CHAPTER 5: SABOTAGE TOOL-KIT

Up to now, we've explored why you choose failure – the hidden desires, comforts, and identity traps. Now it's time to confront how you execute those choices in the practical day-to-day. What are the methods by which you, often cleverly and subtly, sabotage yourself? Every arsonist has a tool-kit: matches, gasoline, rags. Likewise, every self-saboteur (that's been you) has a set of favored tools to set fire to their own plans. It's time to lay out your sabotage tool-kit on the table, one instrument at a time, and recognize them for what they are. Only then can you start removing these tools from your hands.

Let's inventory the common weapons of self-sabotage – see which ones you recognize in yourself:

Procrastination: This is the classic. You delay, delay, delay action on important goals. You tell yourself *"I'll start tomorrow"* while today's opportunity rots. Procrastination gives you immediate relief from anxiety at the cost of future panic. It's a way of failing *slowly*. By not acting, you guarantee that you either rush a poor result at the last minute or miss the boat entirely. Every time you procrastinate, you're essentially deciding to fail in advance – just without admitting it openly. You know this tool well: you've wielded it when you scrolled on your phone for hours instead of working on that project, or when you dawdled until deadlines crushed you. Why do you do it? Because it's easier *now*. Procrastination is comfort-in-the-moment (our old enemy dopamine strikes again). It's the pleasure of *not* doing the hard thing, which your brain rewards instantly. But like a debt, it accumulates interest – the panic and negative consequences later are far worse.

By using procrastination, you've been lighting the fuse on a time-bomb that wrecks your goals.

Perfectionism: Ah yes, the esteemed saboteur wearing a fancy suit. You set unrealistically high standards and tell yourself (and others), *"If it's not perfect, it's not worth doing."* Sounds noble, but it's a *lie*. Perfectionism is just procrastination in a tuxedo. By insisting on perfection, you create an excuse to never finish – or never even start. You perpetually say, *"It's not ready yet,"* and thus you never deliver. Or you avoid taking on challenges because you fear you won't do them perfectly. This tool has a double benefit to the saboteur: it delays action (like procrastination) and protects the ego (because as long as you don't finalize something, you don't have to face it being judged as imperfect). How many projects have you left unfinished in the name of perfection? How many opportunities have you passed up because you didn't feel *perfectly prepared*? Meanwhile, others with half your talent succeeded because they *finished* things and put them out there, flaws and all. You failed by default, polishing your imaginary masterpiece that no one ever sees. Perfectionism as a tool of failure is insidious because it masquerades as a strength. Recognize it: if you truly want success, you must be willing to be imperfect and still push forward.

Distraction & Instant Gratification: You arm yourself with endless distractions – your phone, social media, video games, binge-watching, online shopping, trivial tasks – anything to avoid the real work or difficult reflection. Each time you reach for distraction, you are picking up a tool from the sabotage kit labeled "Dopamine Now, Regret Later." It's as simple as that. For example, instead of studying for two hours, you scroll TikTok for two hours. The immediate effect? Your brain is pleased; it got novelty and little dopamine treats. The delayed effect? You bomb the exam and fail the course. The pattern is clear: you consistently trade long-term achievement for short-term stimulation. It's an addiction like any other. In fact, neuroscientists warn that constant phone use and dopamine hits from social media or games can rewire your brain, lowering your baseline motivation. You become dependent on quick hits and find sustained effort unrewarding. So, distraction isn't just a passive mistake – it's an active self-sabotage tool. Every time you open that app instead of doing what truly matters, you are effectively saying, *"Dear Future Me, screw you. Love, Present Me."* Remember that next time you're tempted to fritter away hours – that temptation is not harmless relaxation; it's self-sabotage with a pretty interface.

Self-Handicapping Behaviors: We touched on this earlier, but let's call them out explicitly. These are deliberate choices to impede your own performance so you have ready excuses. For instance: partying hard the night before a job interview, not reading the instructions on a competition entry, "forgetting" to practice before a performance. By creating an obstacle or neglecting preparation, you ensure that if (when) you fail, you can blame the external factor. It's like a get-out-of-jail-free card for your ego: *"I* *failed, but hey, it's because I was hungover – not because I lack ability."* This tool is particularly cowardly. It's choosing a certain but explainable failure over a possibly devastating attempt at success. Researchers have noted this exact pattern: people will intentionally impede their chances to protect self-esteem in case of failure. It's as if you trip yourself so you can say, "I didn't lose the race because I'm slow; I lost because I tripped." But guess what – you *still* lost the race. And you know you did it to yourself, which deepens the shame long-term, even if it softened the blow in the moment. Throw this tool away. It's better to fail honestly (and learn) than to fail on purpose and learn nothing.

Negative Self-Talk (The Inner Critic): This is the whispering poison you apply to yourself, day in and day out. *"I'm not good enough." "I'll just fail again." "Why bother?" "I'm an imposter."* Every time you indulge these thoughts without countering them, you're using a tool from the kit to chip away at your own confidence and motivation. The inner critic can become so pervasive that it preempts any action: you decide you'll fail *before* you even try, so you don't try (or you sabotage to confirm the belief). It's a self-fulfilling prophecy engine. By believing the worst about yourself, you ensure the worst outcomes. This tool often works in tandem with others: negative self-talk leads to procrastination (because you "know" it won't turn out well), or to distraction (to escape the painful thoughts), or to comfort in the cell ("I suck, might as well not challenge myself"). It's time to realize those negative thoughts are not "truth" – they are a conditioned script. And you've been wielding that script like a weapon against yourself. When such thoughts arise, you must learn to dispute them aggressively or drown them out with action. The longer you let them monologue, the more damage they do.

People-Pleasing and Saying Yes to Everything: How is this self-sabotage? By overcommitting or constantly putting others' priorities before your own, you ensure you have no time or energy left to pursue your goals. It's an indirect method of failure – you fail by *never focusing on your success*. Maybe you say yes to extra work projects, helping friends move, doing favors, attending events you don't care about – all because you can't set boundaries or you fear disappointing people. Meanwhile, your own aspirations gather dust. On the surface, you seem like a generous, busy bee. But underneath, you might be using people-pleasing as a way to avoid the hard work on yourself, or as a way to justify why you're not making progress ("I have no time for my stuff, everyone needs me!"). It's easier to deal with others' requests than to face your own challenges. Recognize this if it's your pattern: are you sabotaging by overload? Trying to be everything for everyone except being great for yourself? Helping others is wonderful, but not when it's a constant escape from helping yourself.

Creating Drama and Conflict: Some self-saboteurs unconsciously stir up interpersonal drama when things are going too smoothly. You might pick fights with your partner or family out of nowhere, or cause issues at work through gossip or argument. Why? Perhaps you thrive on the adrenaline, or you want to externalize your internal turmoil (make outside chaos match inside chaos). But also, it conveniently derails positive momentum. If you were on track with a project, nothing like an emotional blowout to knock you off course. Part of you knows this. So when you sense you're edging toward success or stability (which, as we discussed, might make you uneasy), you ignite a fire elsewhere to distract and sabotage. The result: your focus shifts to the drama, your emotional state is destabilized, and your goal goes unmet. This is a brutal tool because it can damage your relationships deeply. The hidden payoff might be attention (people engage with you through the conflict) or again a reaffirmation of your identity ("See, everything is always a mess in my life"). If you recognize this, you need to address the root – your discomfort with peace and progress – rather than continually blowing up your world.

Choosing the Wrong Allies (Team Sabotage): Sometimes we sabotage ourselves by surrounding with people who we *know* are bad influences or who hold us back. Choosing an unreliable business partner, staying in a friend group that only parties when you're trying to quit drinking, sticking with a toxic mentor who discourages you – these are choices. Perhaps you fear being alone, so you'd rather be in bad company than none. But that bad company drags you down. It provides convenient scapegoats ("It's not me, it's them!") and also feeds the comfort of mediocrity. This overlaps with what's coming in Chapter 6, but it's worth listing here: selecting who is on your "team" is absolutely part of your sabotage tool-kit if you consistently choose folks who enable your worst habits or undermine your progress. It's a tool because it's an action you take to engineer an environment of failure.

Have these hit close to home? Are you wincing with recognition? Good. That discomfort means we're dragging the demons into daylight. The goal here is not to shame you but to identify precisely how you've been doing the devil's work on yourself. You can't fix what you don't see. Now you *see* the arsenal you've been using.

Take a moment and visualize the next time you reach for one of these tools. See it in your mind: You're about to procrastinate – that's like picking up a shiny revolver labeled "delay." You're about to tell yourself you're not good enough – that's like uncapping a bottle of acid labeled "self-doubt" to pour on your confidence. You're about to say yes to something you don't want – that's taking out shackles labeled "overcommitment" to bind your time. Whatever the tool, imagine if in that moment you literally say, "I see what I'm doing. This is sabotage." That act of recognition can be enough to break the pattern then and there. Catching yourself in the act is a huge win.

Now, simply knowing about these tools isn't enough. You have to be prepared to disarm them. That means creating barriers to using them. For example, if distraction is your big one, you might need to physically remove distractions (turn off the phone, use apps to block social media during work hours, etc.). If procrastination is killing you, practice the "two-minute rule" – promise yourself to just start the task for two minutes to overcome inertia. If perfectionism paralyzes you, set hard deadlines and force yourself to deliver draft versions, embracing that they're imperfect. If negative self-talk is rampant, literally start a daily habit of writing counterarguments to those thoughts or use affirmations (and I mean strong, believable ones, not fluffy unicorn stuff) to drown them out.

Each tool has an antidote: procrastination's antidote is action (however small, just start); perfectionism's antidote is embracing *completion over perfection*; distraction's antidote is deliberate focus routines and maybe a *low-dopamine morning* (we'll cover that soon) to break the addiction; self-handicapping's antidote is committing in ways that you *can't* back out (like publicly or with accountability partners); negative self-talk's antidote is intentional self-compassion and evidence-based self-praise (reminding yourself of facts of your capability); people-pleasing's antidote is saying NO and setting clear priorities; drama-stirring's antidote is learning to sit with calm or journal your feelings instead of exploding them outward; bad allies' antidote is *choosing better friends and mentors*, or sometimes walking alone for a while until you find them.

We will delve into environment and group aspects in the next chapter, but it's worth starting to think: how can you restructure your life so that these tools are harder to access? Because when you're tired or stressed, you will reflexively reach for them. The key is to design your routines and environment such that even if you *want* to sabotage, it's a little harder. This gives your higher brain a chance to intervene.

For now, let this chapter's takeaway be crystal clear: **Your failures are not mysteries. They have been engineered by these very tools in your own**

hands. That's the bad news and the good news. Bad because, well, it's been you all along. Good because that means you have the power to stop. You built the fire; you can put it out.

However, there's another dimension we must examine: the *social* dimension. You do not exist in isolation. The people and culture around you have, in subtle and not-so-subtle ways, been keeping that fire of failure lit as well. In the next chapter, *When Teams Love to Lose*, we'll examine how your circle – friends, family, colleagues – might be part of your sabotage cycle, and how to deal with that. Because escaping failure isn't just a solo game; sometimes you have to leave the losing team or change its culture. Let's investigate that now.

CHAPTER 6:
WHEN TEAMS
LOVE TO LOSE

No one fails alone. Even if it feels like a solitary collapse, there are often social forces at play, shaping the context in which you either flourish or flounder. Humans are tribal by nature – we are influenced deeply by those we surround ourselves with. Now it's time to face a hard truth: If you have been chronically failing, chances are you have surrounded yourself with a team that *loves to lose*. Consciously or not, your social circle, family system, or work environment might be reinforcing your will to fail because it suits their comfort or narratives. It's like being on a sports team that's more comfortable with losing because winning would challenge their identity and dynamics.

Think about your circle of friends, your family, your closest colleagues. Do they encourage you to aim higher, or do they subtly pull you back down to earth whenever you try to rise? Sometimes the people who *say* they love us unconsciously want us to stay *small*. Why? Because if one crab escapes the bucket, what do the others do? They pull it back in. Psychologists call this crab mentality – the mindset of "If I can't have it, neither can you.". In a bucket of live crabs, if one tries to climb out, the others will literally grab it and drag it back down, resulting in the entire group's demise. Among humans, this can manifest as members of a group undermining anyone who tries to improve their situation, out of envy, resentment, or fear that they'll be left behind.

Examine if you've been a victim of crab mentality from those around you. Did a friend mock you for deciding to get healthy ("Oh, going to the gym *again*? Don't become one of those fitness snobs.")? Did a sibling roll their eyes when you talked about a professional ambition ("Sure, like *you're* going to start a business.")? Did colleagues discourage you from pushing for a promotion ("Why bother, it's so much extra work, and you might fail.")? These are crabs pulling at you. Sometimes it's not even verbal; it can be subtle cues or a lack of support. You announce a positive change or success, and their response is lukewarm or vaguely negative. Over time, you internalize that staying at their level is what keeps you accepted.

There's also something called *self-evaluation maintenance theory* in social psychology: basically, if someone close to us excels in an area that we also care about, we feel threatened. So we might (often unconsciously) try to downplay their achievements or even hinder them to protect our own self-esteem. Imagine you and your close friend started with similar careers. Suddenly you get a big promotion. If that friend feels left behind, they might begin to undermine you or predict your failure, because your success casts a shadow on their own progress.

THE WILL TO FAIL

It's not a conscious evil plot in most cases – it's a psychological defense. But to you, the effect is the same: negativity, discouragement, or sabotage coming from someone you thought was on your side.

Even families can "love to lose" in a sense. Family roles are a powerful thing: there's the successful one, the funny one, the rebel, the screw-up, etc. If you've long been pegged as the "irresponsible" or "problem" child, and you suddenly try to get your act together, don't be surprised if your family resists it. They might not trust the change ("We'll believe it when we see it"), or they might continually reference your past failures ("Remember when you messed up that other thing..."). Part of them might fear that if you no longer play your role, *their* roles are also called into question. A dysfunctional family often has equilibrium: one person's failures allow others to feel needed, superior, or distracted from their own issues. If you depart from the script, it shakes up the system.

Likewise, consider romantic relationships: an insecure partner might feel threatened if you start improving yourself (getting fit, advancing in career, growing more confident) – they worry you'll outgrow them or attract others. So they may subconsciously sabotage you: maybe by tempting you into breaking your diet or deriding your self-improvement efforts ("Why are you reading those self-help books? You think you're better than me now?"). They might not even realize they're doing it, but they're attempting to keep you as the same person they're comfortable with. They *love* (or need) the version of you that loses or stays stuck, because that version fits their comfort zone.

Group failure can also be cultural. Perhaps you work in a team or company with a toxic culture of learned helplessness – everyone just complains, "This is how it's always been, nothing we do matters." If you come in bright-eyed and wanting to change things, you get smirks and "good luck with that" comments. The group has a shared commitment to failure; success by any member would disrupt the narrative that *it can't be done* or *management is the enemy* or whatever the bonding story is. So they collectively discourage effort. In some workplaces, excelling can even make you a target – coworkers might ostracize you for raising the bar, or try to sabotage your projects out of jealousy. This is crab bucket behavior on an organizational scale.

Sometimes, the team that loves to lose includes *you*. Recall how earlier you might sabotage others who try to climb, because it reflects on you. Are you ever the crab pulling others down? Be honest: did you ever subtly discourage a friend from a big dream because if they succeeded it'd make you feel smaller? Recognizing this tendency in yourself is crucial, because often those dynamics are reciprocal. If you secretly envy your friend's attempt to improve (and maybe undermined it), then likely that friend feels the same towards you and will return the favor of discouragement. Breaking out of a losing team often starts with not participating in the group's negative reinforcement. Stop gossiping, stop one-upping sob stories, stop competing in "who's life is worse"

Olympics. Misery loves company, but you don't have to RSVP to that party.

So what do you do when you realize your social environment is keeping you down? There are two approaches: **change your environment or change your environment.** That's not a typo. It means either *change the people around you* (if possible) or *literally remove yourself and find a new tribe.* The latter is often easier. It's harsh but true that sometimes growth means leaving people behind. You can try to uplift them with you, but they have to be willing. If it's clear they're not, you face a choice: stay and stagnate, or leave and grow.

For example, if your group of friends spends every weekend getting drunk and laughing at any notion of self-betterment, maybe you need to distance yourself and find friends who are on a growth trajectory. If your family constantly drags you into drama or belittles your ambitions, you may need to set firmer boundaries or emotionally detach from their opinions. If a partner truly can't support the better version of you, you may have to evaluate the relationship's future.

Changing your environment doesn't always mean wholesale abandonment of people; it can also mean establishing a new dynamic. Sometimes, communicating your intentions firmly and enlisting support (or at least requesting that they not interfere) can shift things. For instance, telling your friends, "I'm serious about improving this aspect of my life. I understand if it's not your thing, but I'd appreciate you not mocking it and maybe even cheering me on a bit." Good friends will take a hint and might curb the teasing or negativity. They might even be inspired by you eventually. If they don't – if they keep mocking or undermining – then you have your answer: they prefer the losing version of you. That's a friend of your old self, not your new self. You might need to spend less time with them.

It's also worth seeking out new team members – mentors, peers, communities – who embody the attitudes and success you aspire to. Join a club of entrepreneurs if you want to be one. Find an online community about fitness or writing or whatever your goal is. Surround yourself (physically or virtually) with people who are winning or determined to win. Not yes-men or sycophants, but genuine achievers who won't be threatened by your growth – they'll celebrate it, because it aligns with their own path. This does wonders for your mindset. Humans naturally conform to group norms; if you're in a group where excellence is the norm, you'll push yourself to meet it. If you're in a group where complaining is the norm, you'll stay a complainer.

Be mindful: when you start succeeding, you may attract some resentment or attempts to pull you down even from strangers or society at large. Tall poppy syndrome – where people want to cut down those who rise too high – is real. It's visible in social media and public life all the time: the moment someone achieves something, haters come out with negativity. You must develop a thick skin and not internalize that. Learn to expect some resistance when you break out of mediocrity. As the saying goes, "The nail that sticks out gets hammered down." Don't let that scare you; just be ready to dodge some hammers. And remember, many times the "hammer" is just noise from people who don't matter. **Do not let small people keep you from big goals.**

Let's reflect: are there specific people in your life right now whose voice or influence consistently correlates with you staying stuck? Perhaps an old friend who always reminds you of your past failures. Or a colleague who only ever complains and discourages new initiatives. Or a relative who gets uncomfortable if you talk about doing something different from the family norm. Identify them. This doesn't mean you must cut them off entirely (though in extreme cases, you might). It means you consciously adjust how much weight you give their input. Maybe you stop discussing your aspirations with them – share those with someone supportive instead. Maybe you limit time spent engaging in the same old losing activities with them. You don't even have to announce it; just quietly step back and invest more energy elsewhere.

One trap to avoid: don't fall into a martyr or savior complex where you think "I'll succeed and then show them, or then lift them up." Your journey is first and foremost about you. Prove it to *yourself*, not to spite them. And you cannot save people who don't want to be saved. Focus on getting yourself out of the pit; once you're truly clear and strong, you can consider offering a hand – but by then you'll also realize each person must choose to grab it. Some will, some won't.

As you improve, you may indeed lose some relationships. That is sad, but what's sadder is losing *yourself* to keep those relationships. Real friends, real loved ones, will adapt and still love the *real* you, especially as you become a better, happier version. Those who fall away because you're no longer failing? That reveals they were never truly for *you*, just for the comfort you provided them by staying down.

In sum, to break the will to fail, you must sometimes break free from the *network* of failure. Fire those teammates who love to lose, or at least bench them. Draft new players into your life who strive for wins. And importantly, foster an internal team spirit with *yourself* as captain. Decide that even if you stand alone, you'll stand moving forward rather than sitting in a circle of stagnation.

We've now dissected the internal and external mechanics of your self-sabotage. You understand the psychological drives, the personal tools of sabotage, and the social dynamics that kept you failing. This thorough self-confrontation has hopefully lit a new fire in you – not the destructive fire of chaos, but the forging fire of determination.

Now it's time to pivot to solutions – to breaking the circuit of failure and building new circuits of success. In **Part IV: Breaking the Circuit**, we will translate all this insight into concrete changes. We'll start with something as fundamental as your morning and as deep as your brain chemistry (dopamine), and then introduce a concept to recalibrate your tolerance for chaos (the Chaos Baseline Index). These are practical, intense steps to rewire your habits and mindset, forging that mental armor and discipline you need.

You've done the reconnaissance on the enemy (the enemy within and around). Now, soldier, it's time to plan the counterattack. Ready to break the circuit? Let's march into Part IV.

PART IV – BREAKING THE CIRCUIT

CHAPTER 7: LOW-DOPAMINE MORNINGS, HIGH-AGENCY DAYS

Dawn of a new day – in more ways than one. The moment you wake up is when the battle for that day is won or lost. Up until now, you've likely been losing that battle in the first hour without even realizing it. Why? Because you let your primitive cravings run the show from the get-go. Checking your phone notifications immediately, scrolling through a feed while still in bed, slamming caffeine and sugar to shock yourself awake – all these feel normal, but they are kryptonite to your self-discipline. They flood your brain with quick dopamine hits, putting you on a rollercoaster of seeking instant gratification all day. The result? Low willpower, constant distraction, and reinforced habits of procrastination and indulgence. To break the circuit of failure, we're going to start each day by starving those impulses and feeding your agency instead. Enter the concept of low-dopamine mornings.

A "low-dopamine morning" means you deliberately avoid giving your brain easy rewards for the first part of your day. In practice: do not touch that smartphone for at least 30 minutes (and ideally 60) after waking. Avoid the candy-like stimulation of social media, emails, news – anything that delivers a flood of novelty and trivial pleasure straight to your dopamine receptors. Why? Because starting the day with a high spike of dopamine (from those sources) will leave you in a deficit later, craving more stimulation and unable to focus on less immediately exciting tasks. When you delay those digital hits, your focus and productivity will "zoom". It's like training a muscle – you're teaching your brain that it doesn't get dessert before it eats its vegetables.

In place of those instant gratifications, fill your morning with actions that are grounding and intentional: get up and make your bed, drink a glass of water (throw a pinch of salt in it for electrolytes if you want to follow Andrew Huberman's tip), move your body (stretching, a short walk outside, or a quick exercise routine). If possible, step outside and let natural daylight hit your eyes for 5-10 minutes soon after waking; this isn't pop wellness – neuroscientists confirm morning sunlight helps regulate your circadian rhythm and hormones, enhancing alertness and mood. Notice, none of these are giving you a *dopamine spike* in the way checking social media or chugging a sugary coffee would. They are relatively low-stimulation, physical activities. This is exactly the point.

By doing this, you achieve two things: **First**, you start the day in control. You tell your brain what we're doing, rather than letting the phone or the news hijack your agenda with anxiety or entertainment. You are proactively setting the tone. This builds a sense of agency – the feeling that *you* are the commander of your day. **Second**, you keep your dopamine levels stable and modest in the morning, which paradoxically leads to *higher* sustained motivation and energy later. Think of dopamine like a budget: spend it all in one go early (via Instagram, sugary breakfast, etc.), and you'll be bankrupt by midday – lethargic, unfocused, craving another hit. But if you save and invest it gradually, you have steady drive throughout the day.

Scientists like Dr. Huberman emphasize avoiding what he calls "dopamine stacking" early in the day – combining multiple pleasurable stimuli – because it leads to a crash and a state of *underwhelm* where nothing feels satisfying. For example, if you wake up, immediately blast music, scroll social media, and eat a pastry, you've layered several dopamine sources. You might feel great for an hour, then motivation tanks. Alternatively, a low-dopamine morning might feel a bit bland initially, but by midday, you find that doing a challenging task feels *rewarding* (because you haven't drowned your brain in artificial rewards already). You've essentially allowed your brain chemistry to align actual accomplishment with dopamine release, rather than cheap stimuli. In short: **discipline in the morning creates freedom in the day**.

Now, let's acknowledge something: the first few times you attempt a low-dopamine morning, you will feel a bit restless or irritable. You're used to immediate hits – the quick glance at messages, the coffee with two sugars, the morning TV or YouTube routine. When you cut those out, your brain goes "Wait, where's my fun?!" That discomfort is a good sign – it means you're training the "warlike" part of you to sit still and take orders for once. Embrace it as the feeling of breaking chains. Within a week or two of consistent practice, you'll start noticing clearer focus and a surprising sense of calm drive in the morning. Many who adopt this approach report that not only do they get more done, but they feel less anxious and more in control.

Concrete steps to implement starting tomorrow morning:

No Phone Upon Waking: If your phone is your alarm, fine – turn off the alarm and then *do not* open any apps. Better yet, get a cheap alarm clock and charge your phone outside the bedroom at night. Physically removing the temptation is half the battle. The world will survive without you for one hour each morning, I promise. The messages and feeds will be there later. Consider it a sacred hour for yourself.

Hydrate and Expose to Light: Drink a tall glass of water to rehydrate your brain and body (you dehydrate overnight). If daylight is accessible, get some; if not, turn on bright lights. Light tells your body it's time to be alert. Some also swear by stepping outside for a few minutes even if it's chilly – the combination of light and fresh air is a natural stimulant that wakes you *without* adrenaline-jacking anxiety.

Physical Movement: Do some form of movement. It could be exercise (push-ups, a quick jog, yoga, etc.) or as simple as doing your morning hygiene routine vigorously (yes, even a thorough face wash and stretching can count). Movement triggers the release of dopamine and norepinephrine gradually, boosting your mood and focus for hours. Andrew Huberman's research even highlights that certain "good stress" like cold exposure or intense exercise early can elevate dopamine significantly *and* sustain it without a crash. For example, a 1-minute cold shower might sound like hell, but it can spike dopamine by up to 2.5x baseline and keep it up for hours – leaving you in an energized, motivated state. That is a far more useful dopamine elevation than the quick blip from checking Facebook.

Mindful Planning or Journaling: Instead of consuming content, produce something, even if it's just words on a page for yourself. Write down your top 1-3 priorities for the day. Or jot a few lines of reflection – maybe an affirmation of who you want to be today (aligned with the new identity you're forging). This sets intention. It literally takes 5 minutes, but it primes your brain to focus on what matters, not whatever shiny thing the world throws at you. It's you telling your brain, "Here's our mission for today."

Delay Caffeine (Optional but Powerful): If you're a coffee or tea drinker, try waiting 60-90 minutes after waking to have it. Why? Your body naturally releases cortisol (a wake-up hormone) in the morning; caffeine immediately can blunt that natural process and also lead to a bigger afternoon crash once it wears off. By waiting, you allow your body to fully wake up on its own, and then caffeine when you truly need it will be more effective. Also, caffeine does trigger dopamine (that's partly why it feels good). Delaying it means your dopamine morning remains low. When you do consume it, it's mid-morning – aligning with when your focus might naturally dip a bit. Many high performers do this and find it extends their morning energy significantly. Try it. At first you might feel a bit zombie-like for that first hour without coffee, but you'll adapt, and the payoff is smoother energy.

The above routine, or some variant of it, should take maybe 30-60 minutes. This is your armor donning ritual each day. You are essentially putting on mental armor against distraction and reactivity. The warlike part of you is being directed towards constructive habits (movement, planning) instead of self-destructive ones.

By the time you do eventually check your phone or email, you'll notice something: it has less of a hold on you. You won't get as easily sucked into an hour of scrolling because you've already started the day on *your* terms and accomplished a few things. You have momentum. You have agency. It's like you've planted your flag and now the rest of the day must work around *you*, not vice versa. Contrast this with rolling over and immediately drowning in the phone – starting the day reactive, likely seeing some news or message that puts you in a comparative, anxious, or distracted state. No wonder so many days used to slip from your grasp by noon.

This practice also bleeds into the rest of your day. A low-dopamine morning often leads to more mindful dopamine management overall. You may find it easier to say no to distractions later, because you set a precedent of discipline. It's a cascade of positive effects: strong morning = strong day = good sleep = better next morning, and so on. You begin an upward spiral, the opposite of the downward spiral you'd been caught in.

Now, a caution: implementing a morning routine alone is not a panacea. It's one crucial piece, but by itself won't solve everything. However, it is disproportionately important because it addresses the root *state* from which you operate. You can think of it this way: Previously, you've been starting the day on the back foot, fighting uphill against your own chemically induced lethargy and distraction. Now, you start on the front foot, proactive and aligned. It makes tackling all your other changes and goals easier.

Also, "morning" is whenever you wake. If you have a night shift or unusual schedule, the principle remains – the first hour of your day, whenever that is, should follow these low-dopamine, high-agency guidelines.

As you incorporate this, be as consistent as you can. There will be days you slip – you grab the phone or oversleep. Don't let one slip become an excuse to abandon it ("ah, I failed today, might as well doomscroll for an hour"). Every day is a new battle. Win it anew. And when you see the benefits stacking – maybe you realize you've had five days of doing what you *planned* to do without so much inner resistance – celebrate that. That's evidence of the circuit breaking.

Remember: your mornings set the neural tone for your days. Turn those quiet early hours into a training ground for your willpower. Make them almost monk-like: simple, purposeful, disciplined. In a peaceful morning, you're forging the weapons you'll use to slay the dragons of the day.

With your mornings handled, we move to another

deeply ingrained factor: your baseline need for chaos and intensity. We touched on it earlier with the chaos addiction and being uncomfortable with stability. Now let's formalize a concept to measure and adjust it: I call it the **Chaos Baseline Index (CBI)**. It's time to quantify and then lower the chaos you consider normal in your life so that calm and focus can reign, allowing sustained success. Let's dive into that next.

CHAPTER 8:
THE CHAOS
BASELINE INDEX

How much chaos can you handle before you freak out? And conversely, how much calm can you handle before you *create* chaos? These questions point to a sort of internal set point: your comfort level with disorder versus order, crisis versus peace. I call this your **Chaos Baseline Index (CBI)**. It's a personal metric, an index of how much chaotic energy – drama, urgency, instability – you are accustomed to and subconsciously seek. High CBI individuals thrive in turmoil and feel anxious in calm. Low CBI individuals feel at ease in stability and are disturbed by chaos. The problem is, if you've had a will to fail, your CBI is likely sky-high. You're so used to chaos that you generate it when it's lacking. To break the circuit of self-sabotage, we need to *lower* your CBI dramatically.

First, identify where you might stand. Do you find yourself *bored* or *uneasy* when life goes smoothly? As earlier chapters uncovered, many with a history of self-sabotage do. One woman described how stability felt so unsettling to her that she would overthink and cause problems just because things being calm made her anxious. She admitted that if everything seemed fine, she'd *subconsciously look to create some sort of problem*. That's a prime example of a high CBI – she literally couldn't handle a calm life without trying to raise the chaos level. Another sign: perhaps you procrastinate until an emergency is upon you because you subconsciously need that adrenaline (chaos) to get anything done. Or you routinely double-book yourself, run late, or create mini-crises like misplacing items, forgetting deadlines – it's almost as if you ensure something is on fire at all times.

Now ask: what was your formative environment? Did you grow up in unpredictability – perhaps financial instability, or fighting in the household, or frequent moves, or a volatile parent? If yes, you likely internalized that *as normal*. As an adult, when things are stable, some part of you might still be bracing for impact, and if none comes, you produce it. You might even equate calm with boredom or emptiness. Conversely, if you grew up in a very stable environment but later experienced chaos (say in a toxic relationship or a stint in a high-stress job), you might have developed a taste for it then. Everyone's calibration is different, but awareness is key.

We will treat CBI like we would treat any baseline: by gradually adjusting it and tracking progress. Imagine someone who lives near a train track. Initially, the noise is jarring, but over time, that becomes baseline – they hardly notice trains blaring. Take them to the quiet countryside, and the silence might actually feel eerie to them. Their baseline for noise is high. But if they *stay* in the quiet long enough, they'll recalibrate; they'll start noticing and appreciating subtle sounds, and a train would again become unbearable. Our goal is to do this with the noise (chaos) in your life.

Step 1: Measure Your Current CBI. This isn't a precise science, but you can do a qualitative assessment. Reflect on the past week or two. How many chaotic events occurred (crises, dramas, last-minute scrambles)? How many were avoidable or self-inflicted? For each day, give it a chaos score from 1 to 10 (1 = totally peaceful, everything as planned; 10 = total shitstorm). Be honest – and factor in internal chaos too (an anxious breakdown might count as chaos even if outward events were fine). Now, what's your average? Let's say you're averaging a 7 – meaning there's a moderate drama or rush daily. That's your current CBI in practice. If you find more than one or two days a week hitting high chaos (7+), and rarely any days at 1-2, you indeed have a high baseline.

Also note how you felt on the lower chaos days.

Did you feel strange or restless when things went according to plan? That's a sign your baseline expects more chaos. One might find they actually *introduce* some on a calm day by say, reading upsetting news or stirring an argument or suddenly doubting a decision and creating an internal conflict – all because subconsciously, "it's too quiet, something must be wrong." A telling exercise is to deliberately do nothing for an hour (no phone, no tasks, just sit or walk quietly) and see if you can stand it. If it drives you nuts, your baseline tolerance for calm is low.

Step 2: Set a Target for Lower Chaos. This might mean aiming for more days that are, say, 3 or below on that chaos scale, and fewer at 7+. Another way: aim to increase the longest stretch of calm you can handle. For example, maybe you realize you haven't had a single day in months without something blowing up. Try to achieve one completely uneventful day – and notice how it feels. It might actually feel uncomfortable! But that's the discomfort of growth.

Step 3: Proactively Reduce Chaos Factors. Look at your life and identify sources of recurring chaos. Some chaos comes at us externally, but often we have more control than we admit. Common sources and fixes:

Disorganization: If you're always losing keys, forgetting deadlines, rushing last minute – implement structure. Set up a key hook, use a planner with reminders, prep things the night before. Organization is the nemesis of chaos. Initially, it will feel tedious if you're not used to it. But remember, you're retraining your baseline. Organized = calm, predictable days.

Overcommitment: If you're juggling too much, you ensure chaos because you'll constantly be dropping balls or sprinting between commitments. Start saying "no" more. Cancel or postpone non-essential stuff. Give yourself buffers between tasks/ meetings. A less packed schedule automatically lowers daily chaos.

Toxic People or Drama-Inducing Contacts: Are

there individuals who regularly bring drama into your life? Limit exposure. If someone is always in crisis and dragging you in, set boundaries. You might have a friend who loves to call with emergencies that really aren't – lovingly step back a bit. You can care without being enmeshed.

Digital Chaos: Endless notifications, news alerts, social media rabbit holes – these create a sense of chaos and urgency. Turn off non-critical notifications. Check news once a day at most, not every hour. Curate your online feeds to avoid outrage-bait content that spikes your adrenaline. The world's madness doesn't have to infect your mind constantly.

Environments: A cluttered, noisy environment can keep you on edge. Take time to tidy your living/work space. A clean, organized space promotes calm. If your environment is literally loud (roommates shouting, TV blaring, etc.), invest in earplugs or negotiate quiet hours.

Habits: Look at habits that generate chaos: waking up late (morning chaos), not meal planning (leads to frantic unhealthy eating or going hungry then binging), leaving things to the last minute (deadline panics). Implement the opposite habits gradually (get up on time, plan meals, chip away at tasks early).

Step 4: Tolerate Calm in Gradual Doses. Reducing chaos isn't just about subtracting stressors, it's about *adding* calm and learning to be okay with it. If you're not used to peaceful periods, you have to expose yourself to them like a therapy. For instance, schedule an evening where you *don't* fill it with any drama or stimulation – maybe you read a book or take a slow walk. Initially you might feel *"I should be doing something!"* or your mind might conjure worries to create chaos. Resist the urge to add chaos. Just observe the discomfort, breathe through it, and continue with calm. Over time, your nerves adapt, and you'll start to find these calm moments not only bearable but actually pleasant and recharging.

One helpful tool is mindfulness or meditation. If you can sit with your breath for 10 minutes a day, you're effectively lowering internal chaos voluntarily.

You learn that a thought or urge for drama arises, and you don't have to follow it – you can just let it pass. It's weight training for tolerating stillness. There's a reason many high-performing people (who handle massive external chaos calmly) have a meditation practice – it inoculates them against being reactive.

Step 5: Track Progress and Reward It. Since we made CBI somewhat numerical, use that. Maybe keep a simple journal where at day's end, you jot a chaos score and note what happened. If you had a mild day (score 3) and you *didn't* sabotage it, that's a win – circle it. If you maintained calm through something that would've normally thrown you, note that. Conversely, if you see you triggered chaos out of habit, identify it: "Got anxious nothing was happening, so I texted an ex I shouldn't have – chaos ensued." That's a pattern to cut off next time. Over a few weeks, aim to see the average score go down or at least the number of high-chaos spikes reduced.

Also, find healthy ways to get *positive* excitement or stimulation so your brain doesn't feel starved and revert to chaos. This could be intense exercise, creative work, or scheduled adventurous activities like rock climbing on weekends – something that gives a dopamine and adrenaline rush in a controlled, beneficial way. Essentially, you consciously fulfill that warlike need for intensity in arenas that don't wreck your life. If you give your inner adrenaline-junkie a healthier outlet, it won't go joyriding through your personal life causing drama.

Be prepared for some pushback – both internally and externally. Internally, as mentioned, you might feel uneasy when things go well. It might even feel like vulnerability. Some people are so used to chaos that calm feels like standing naked and exposed. You're used to fighting fires, and when there's no fire, you start wondering, *Who am I if not a crisis manager?* Stick with it; that's just the old identity and baseline complaining (like an addict missing their fix). Externally, if you stop engaging in the usual drama, people around you may notice. They might think you're being cold or distant if you don't react as before. That's okay. You can explain if needed: "I'm trying to stress less and focus more on what matters, so I'm not getting into X like I used to." You don't owe anyone an apology for preserving your sanity.

Lowering your CBI is basically about teaching yourself that *peace is not boring or dangerous – it's the platform for growth and joy.* When you aren't busy extinguishing self-lit fires, you have energy to build something: your craft, your career, your relationships, your health. Peace is fertile soil. As you acclimate to a lower chaos life, you'll likely discover levels of focus, creativity, and even happiness that were previously unreachable amid the noise.

Remember the quote from earlier: people who know only chaos find stability threatening. We are flipping that narrative: you will know chaos *for what it is* – a toxin – and find stability satisfying. Instead of craving the rollercoaster, you'll find fulfillment in the steady climb.

There's one more facet to breaking the circuit we should cover. You've strengthened your mornings (personal discipline) and lowered your chaos baseline (environmental stability). These set the stage. Now the final chapter is about fully *choosing* and committing to the new orientation of your will. You've starved the will to fail of fuel; now you must feed and ignite the **will to forge** – to create, to overcome, to truly live. It's time to convert all this inner work into a forward-driving philosophy for the rest of your life. On to the final part, where we go from failing to forging.

PART V – CHOOSING THE OTHER WILL

CHAPTER 9: FROM WILL TO FAIL TO WILL TO FORGE

You stand at a crossroads now. On one side is the familiar path, well-trodden by your past self: the path of the will to fail. It's littered with your previous footsteps, looping in circles, leading to dead ends. On the other side is a new path, uncharted territory for you: the path of the **will to forge**. To "forge" is to form, create, and shape with force and fire. It implies both heat and perseverance – just as metal is forged in flames, you will forge a new life through the trials you face, rather than being destroyed by them. This is Michel's most assertive call to you: to *redirect* that powerful will of yours that once unconsciously sought failure, and aim it, consciously, at building and conquering.

Up till now, your will has been like a double-edged sword you turned against yourself. You had a warlike spirit (the part Nietzsche identified), but under peace you attacked yourself. Now, you're going to harness that same fighting spirit and aim it outward – to cut through obstacles, not self-sabotage. The intensity doesn't go away; it gets *reassigned*. The aggression you directed inward out of lack of external challenge – you will now direct it at the real challenges that matter: achieving your goals, standing up for your values, pushing through discomfort to grow.

Think of Freud's concept of the death drive we discussed. He said there's a drive toward destruction in us. Well, perhaps that can never be fully eliminated – but it can be rechanneled. Instead of destroying yourself, destroy the impediments in your life. Destroy ignorance with knowledge. Destroy weakness with training. Destroy procrastination with action. In doing so, you aren't feeding the death drive in the literal sense, you're transforming its energy into life-affirming accomplishments. It's like psychological alchemy: turning lead into gold, turning self-destructive impulses into self-constructive outcomes.

Recall the notion of Eros vs Thanatos – life instinct vs death instinct. By choosing the will to forge, you are consciously siding with Eros. You are pledging allegiance to the part of you that wants to live fully, create, love, and leave a mark, rather than the part that wants to shrink, hide, and end things. This might sound abstract, but it's deeply practical: every day, in each choice, you ask yourself – does this action align with the life-building me or the life-destroying me? Choose life. Choose building. Choose forging.

It's crucial to understand that forging is *active*. It's not passive endurance; it's a fight. The will to forge is not about having an easy life – it's about attacking life's difficulties head on to shape something meaningful out of them. Nietzsche famously talked about *amor fati* – love of fate, meaning loving whatever happens to you because it's fuel for your growth. A forging mindset says: *Whatever happens, even failures and pain, I will use it. I will make it forge me rather than break me.* If you slip up and sabotage one day, you don't spiral into "Oh see, I failed again." No, you analyze it as useful data: why did I slip? What can I do differently? In this way, even setbacks become part of the forging process, hammering you into a sharper sword.

The will to forge also means embracing responsibility. Earlier, we hammered the point that you must own your failures. Likewise, you must own your successes and, beyond that, *own your mission.* No one is coming to hand you purpose or drive. You decide it. This is where you ask the big question: *What am I going to forge? What life, what self, what legacy?* It could be as straightforward as "I will forge a career I'm proud of and raise my family with love," or as grand as "I will change the world in this specific way." The key is that it's *yours* and it inspires you enough to keep you focused. The will to fail was directionless – it just avoided and destroyed. The will to forge needs direction – a vision of what you're building so you can channel your energy toward it.

Let's make it concrete: Suppose you always had a dream to, say, write a novel, but you self-sabotaged it for years. Embracing will to forge, you say: "Enough. I'm going to write it. It might suck initially, but I will forge it through drafts and edits. I will face the discomfort and finish." Now each morning you get up and you write, as an act of will. You stop saying, "I wish I could" and you start saying "I *am* doing it." You see yourself as a creator, not a consumer of pity. This psychological shift is huge.

Or, suppose you've long struggled with fitness and health, always falling back into poor habits. Will to forge says: "My body is my forge and I am the blacksmith. Through discipline and sweat, I'll forge strength and vitality." That means when you're tired and hearing the old voice, "skip the workout," the new will steps in and says "No. This discomfort is the hammer and flame – by enduring it I become stronger." You almost revel in the challenge because you know it's shaping you. Instead of, "I can't believe I have to do this," it becomes, "I choose to do this because it's turning me into who I want to be."

It's an intense mindset, yes. Serious, judgmental, and harsh, as we set out to maintain in tone. The will to forge does not coddle you. It's that stern inner coach or drill sergeant that doesn't accept your excuses because it sees your potential. Under conditions of peace (when things are easy), the warlike man previously attacked himself; now, under conditions of challenge, the warlike *still attacks* – but he attacks the challenge, not himself. He thrives in productive struggle. He wages war for his dreams instead of sabotaging them.

Remember our earlier discussions on dopamine and motivation, on harnessing those for sustained effort? The will to forge plugs right into that. You're delaying gratification willingly because you're after the bigger reward. It's like a blacksmith in a forge – it's hot, sweaty, and you're striking metal repeatedly. Not comfortable, but you're focused on the end product –

THE WILL TO FAIL

a fine sword or tool. You need that vision of the result to keep you going through the sparks and heat.

This final rallying chapter must emphasize: *This is a choice.* Possibly the most important choice of your life. No one can make it for you. You choose, here and now, to redirect your will. To declare internally: **I will no longer be my own enemy. I will be my own warrior.** The time for pity parties is over. The time for half-measures and timid attempts is over. You have stared your self-sabotage in the face and you're disgusted by it. Good. Now channel that disgust not into self-hatred, but into determination. Be almost *angry* in a productive way: angry at the years wasted, and absolutely unwilling to waste a year more.

Transformation isn't magic; it's forged piece by piece. You will have to reaffirm this choice often, perhaps daily. Some mornings the old lethargy will whisper, "Does it really matter? Just stay the same." That's when you roar back: "I refuse to fail by default. I refuse to be less than I could be." And then you act – you do something concrete that the old you would avoid. With each such action, you're forging neural pathways of success, grit, and resilience.

To keep yourself true on this new path, it's helpful to articulate *principles* or a personal manifesto. For instance:

"I take ownership of every outcome – no more victim mindset."

"I seek the truth, especially about myself, even when it's hard."

"I finish what I start, unless a conscious strategic decision to pivot."

"I do what I say I will do – to myself and others."

"I surround myself with people and inputs that elevate me, and distance myself from those that don't."

"I convert pain into power, not into self-pity. Every setback teaches me and fuels me."

"I choose long-term meaning over short-term comfort, every time."

Write your own and read them. Memorize them. These are like the blacksmith's code of practice in the forge of life.

Is this a lot? Yes. But ultimately, the concept is simple: Stop using your will against yourself; start using it *for* yourself. All the research, philosophy, and neuroscience we have considered all point to the tremendous power within you, and how it can go awry or be set right. Nietzsche knew humans had a deep will to power and overcoming; Freud knew we wrestle with drives that can undo us; modern science shows our brain will follow whatever we train it to pursue (chaos or creation). So now you have to decide which master you'll serve.

Let's be clear: The will to fail will not disappear overnight. It's a pattern, an old groove. It will try to reassert itself cunningly. But every time it does is another chance to strengthen the will to forge by rejecting the old way. In time, the balance shifts. You'll notice you haven't self-sabotaged in a while, that you're quicker to catch negative spirals, that you bounce back faster, that you no longer fear success – in fact you *expect* it, because you trust yourself to handle it. You'll have a track record of following through, of facing fears. Success breeds success; confidence compounds. And those around you? They'll notice. Some will not like the new you – usually those who remain stuck themselves. But many will be inspired or at least respectful. You might even end up leading others by example, even if quietly, showing what it looks like to step out of the self-made prison.

By forging yourself anew, you give others permission to do the same. You become proof that even deeply ingrained self-sabotage can be overcome. People might start asking, "How did you turn things around?" And you can share some of this manifesto: the brutal honesty, the hidden payoff exposé, the war on morning indulgences, the chaos reduction, and ultimately the choice to fight for oneself rather than against.

As you conclude this work, let's revisit the image of you in a forge. The air is hot, the anvil is before you, hammer in hand. The raw material is your life

– all your experiences, talents, scars, and hopes. The fire is your intense emotion – your anger at past failures, your desire for better, your passion. The hammer is your daily actions, each swing shaping the metal. And the will to forge is the arm lifting and swinging that hammer relentlessly. You strike, and strike, and strike again. Sparks fly – those are challenges and pain, but you don't fear them; they light your workshop. The noise is loud – that's the sound of breaking old patterns. And with each blow, something solid, sharp, and gleaming takes form. It is *you* – the new you, a weapon forged from what was once scrap.

In a famous quote: "The same boiling water that softens the potato hardens the egg." The circumstances can either break you or make you – it's your inner composition that decides. By altering your will, you change your composition. The heat of life will now harden and temper you, not turn you to mush.

The will to fail is a slow death by a thousand

cuts. The will to forge is life grabbed by the collar and lived with fierce intentionality. It will not always be easy – in fact, it's guaranteed not to be, and that's fine. You aren't asking for easy anymore; you're asking for *worth it*. Under the conditions of peace, you once attacked yourself; now, under conditions of challenge, you revel in attacking the challenge. Under the lure of comfort, you once wilted; now, you resist and grow. Under the weight of identity, you once sank; now, you break old identities and shape new ones.

No more will to fail. That was the old story. Close that book. Burn it if you must. From here on, your life is an act of forging. You shape yourself and your world with the fires of effort and the blows of steadfast action. And when the final chapters of your life are written, let it not be said that you *collapsed* under your own sabotage, but rather that you rose, battle-scarred and unbowed, having turned every curse into a blessing, every weakness into strength, and every failure into fuel.

This is your mandate now. No looking back. Take one step on the new path, and then another. Feel that rush? That's your will coming alive, this time aligned with your highest self. Keep going. Build momentum. The days of being your own worst enemy are done – you are now your own commander, protector, and creator. The will to fail is dead; *long live the will to forge.*

Go forth and forge your destiny. The fire is waiting, and so is the world. Make the choice, every day, every moment – and never, ever, give that will up again.

Your life is yours to shape. Seize it. Forge it.